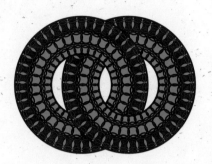

The One Fifteen to Penn Station

To Natalie,
thanks for coming

The One Fifteen
to Penn Station

KEVIN CAREY

Kevin McCoy

Salem State
9/20/12

CavanKerry ◊ Press LTD.

CavanKerry Press Ltd.
Fort Lee, New Jersey
www.cavankerrypress.org

Library of Congress Cataloging-in-Publication Data

Carey, Kevin, 1957-
The one fifteen to Penn Station / Kevin Carey. -- 1st ed.
   p. cm.
ISBN-13: 978-1-933880-29-7 (alk. paper)
ISBN-10: 1-933880-29-5 (alk. paper)
I. Title.

PS3603.A7416O54 2012
811'.6--dc23

2011051214

Cover photograph by Michaela Carey
Cover and interior design by Gregory Smith
First Edition 2012, Printed in the United States of America

CavanKerry Press is dedicated to springboarding the careers of previously unpublished poets by bringing to print two to three New Voices annually. Manuscripts are selected from open submission; CavanKerry Press does not conduct competitions.

CavanKerry Press is grateful for the support it receives from the New Jersey State Council on the Arts.

To my old Headmaster and anyone who cares,
before I go, I'd like to say my prayers

—Ian Anderson

for Betty, Kevin, and Michaela

Contents

Contents

Foreword

More than ten years ago I sponsored an exhibit by the sculptor Henri Simon at the Broadway Gallery of Passaic County Community College in Paterson, New Jersey. As part of the exhibit, we displayed a large copper sculpture of a Model T Ford, complete with a battery, ignition key, hood, fenders, and wheels. It was shiny and perfect. The students couldn't stay away from it. They were fascinated by its polished presence in the center of the Gallery. The only thing wrong with it is that it didn't run. For me, much of contemporary poetry has the same problem; it's shiny and beautiful with its polished language and elegant lines. What it is missing, however, is the ability to move us to laughter or tears or smiles.

Reading Kevin Carey's *The One-Fifteen to Penn Station* gives me hope that one can craft a poem and not lose the heart of it, the quality that touches us and forms a bridge between the poet and the reader.

Carey's poems, firmly rooted in the American landscape of the city and its surrounding towns, bring these places and people alive for us in poetry that is specific, clear, and unflinching. Whether he is describing the scene he sees outside the train window in all its gritty, surprising beauty or working-class Revere Beach, the town where he grew up and where his mother still lives, or the thirty-five foot Madonna on a hill in East Boston, his observations are precise, his humor sardonic, his eyes are the window through which we observe the world he knows so well.

Carey's universe may be set in blue-collar New England, but out of that backdrop, we find a man very much like ourselves trying to hold on to what everyone loses eventually— his children as they grow up, his parents, long-time friends, perhaps, most important of all, his sense of where he thought he was going to be when he was young and what life is for him now, a middle-aged man searching and asking why some of our best intentions go wrong. The poems are muscular, rooted, and blunt but move forward with an energy that cannot disguise the essential vulnerability. They have that quality of sustained attention, of life deeply lived and felt, that makes them an exploration of all that it means to be human, to want more than we have been given, yet grateful for the moments of grace and connection that transform us.

—Maria Mazziotti Gillan

The One Fifteen
to Penn Station

Kevin Carey

The One Fifteen to Penn Station

— wrote on a train

Ten minutes out of Back Bay Station
and I am reminded of a long-ago train
and the futile mission I was on then
and where it brought me and why
it cornered me into thinking I was
onto something, something more
than the wrong hard turn that left me
high but hungry and hurt,
and when I woke up I realized
some things can't ever be fixed
no matter how hard you try.

The tracks connect us like telephone lines
and power grids and graffiti walls
and parking lots and barbed wire
and chain link and churches,
miles and miles of churches,
and acres of trees flipping by my window
like the clips of conversation around me.

You can see it all out a train window,
you can see the signs: *checks cashed,
cold beer, rooms by week, shows nightly,
hawk here, bet here, pay for junk here,*
the spray paint broken glass plywood walls,
make peace, Jesus saves, funk lives,
the clothesline, the cardboard,
the vapid faces of the children,
long lines of blank-faced children,
and it reminds you how easy it is

to walk a mile like a rummy in both directions,
run farther and farther away and closer to yourself,
until the worst bet becomes the only one left
and the trouble follows you like soup cans
tied to a wedding car.

But sometimes you catch a glimpse
of a hundred sparrows bursting
from the cover of a lonely maple tree,
or some kid hitting a rubber fastball
high over the telephone wire in slow motion,
or you pass a man standing in a junkyard
pointing to the bottom of a scrap pile,
and you think no matter where you go
you're always trying to get to the bottom
of the junk,
the junk you choose,
the junk you hide from,
the junk that keeps you riding the rails,

and the train sneaks into the city,
as if someone left the back door open.

A Well-Oiled Machine

It used to work just fine
day in and day out
it was a well-oiled machine
no glitches in the system
except for those times it got too oiled
and couldn't function after.
Then it made a big mistake
it added things to itself
things like existential thought
and Plato and Buddhist meditation
things that were new and didn't belong
and the machine started to slow
started to look at its parts
what factory they came from
where they were made
where they would go when they finally broke
and the answers mucked up the gears
and the machine stopped working
and it wanted to know why it worked
in the first place
and for what reason
and for how long
and bit by bit the machine got dusty
and gathered rust and spent all day reading Chekhov
in the corner of an empty factory.

The Road Narrows

I believe Jesus comes out at night
and sits on a hill in East Boston
beneath the thirty-five-foot madonna
and wonders why people can't believe
his mother was like any other—
suffering the pains of birth, the grief
of losing a son, the sweet gift of
desire in creating one.

I believe he looks over the Mystic River
and sees the road narrow beyond the curve
of the Central Artery and thinks to himself—
how is it I can't see the suffering from here?

I believe he looks at the evening traffic
curled into lanes along the Big Dig,
the lights left on along Storrow Drive,
and realizes his magic only works
sleight of hand in close quarters.

When I was an altar boy I snuck
into the sacristy and poured a goblet
of Father Messina's wine, and drank
alone with the ghosts of the stations,
and a few mice looking for scraps
from the bake sale.

I got warm in the belly and stepped
slowly and slurred my words
and giggled at things that seemed funny,
even if they weren't.

The church baptized me, the church
— goes from life to death
married me, the church buried my father,
and still I wonder if the archangels
of stolen wine have tracked me down
and come to claim their sacred vessels.

Still I wonder why Jesus can't tell people
his mother was a real woman,
still I wonder why I can't see the suffering
in time to stop it.

And from high on a hill the only thing I know
is that the road narrows until it is out of sight,
away and alone, like the birds that take flight
from the great statues in the sky,
like the spirits of unguarded sacristies,
like the prayers of young children
hidden beyond the highways of the cities
of the world,
believing in every invention but their own.

Crazy Stuff

I hold your hand while you sleep,
your swollen fingers squeezing mine.
There's a football game on TV,
orange Syracuse jerseys covered in mud
the way we saw ourselves playing,
rainy days on the side lawn in the fall,
while you watched from the kitchen window.
You wake for a moment and I ask you how you feel,
your eyes fogged and far away,
and I remember what we talked about,
the doctors, my mother, God.
"Do you believe in God?" I asked
"Sure," you said, like why not or who doesn't,
and the few days before that when I told you
"I'm sorry for all the crazy stuff, it must have
been hard."
You clutch my hand
like a frightened, fevered child
holding for a breath that might not return,
and I am reminded of Lucinda Williams,
a Lake Charles country song,
and the angel at your ear
in those long last moments.

Frozen Peas

Some nights the other offices are empty
no phones ringing
no people yelling at their psychotherapists
and I drink tea and read crime fiction
and leave the groceries defrosting in the car
by the soot-topped snowbanks.
Some nights I hear the homeless guys
pulling at the lobby door hoping
for a chance to hide in the basement,
or the large lady down the hall
calling the cops on them.
Some nights the heat kicks on
and the radiator sprays steam
onto the cracked walls behind it,
partially painted yellow where the brush could reach.
Some nights I can't read
and I stare at the dirty fan blades spinning
above my children's paintings
like an old movie I watch over and over
because it reminds me of something from before
and if I shut the door tight I can pretend,
some nights,
that time isn't passing too quickly
that there's enough of it to do everything I want to do
and some nights I'm not afraid
but in the flow of life's traffic
like the cars on the highway by my house
where they drive all night and never stop
and some nights I feel like I can freeze it,
right where it is,

my moment hidden away in my office
hand in hand with the grand design
or the mystery that keeps us all on the same page
and some nights I sit and try to remember
the pages I just turned
calculating the days I need to live
to be as old as my mother
and while I sit and read and stare
and think and sneak away from life
the groceries in my car keep defrosting,
french fries melting to their former self
peas thawing through their frosted coats as if
they weren't supposed to touch.

—Imagery / Relatable

Revere Beach

Once they charged to see a train wreck on Side
Beach, watched horses diving thirty feet into a pool,
paid five cents to look at premature babies
in incubators. As a teenager I saw the last
remnants of the arcades, one wooden
roller coaster they tried ten times to burn
to the ground, and the rotating neon line
of barrooms - the Ebb Tide, the Mickey Mouse,
Sammy's Patio, the rock and roll, the disco,
the punk, the bikers, the strippers, the wise
guys.

I worked this beach, played this beach,
passed out drunk and bleeding on this beach,
in the shadow of the gray Boston skyline,
at the foot of the General Edwards Bridge,
where we crossed as kids to sit on the fence
of the drive-in and smoke weed and run from
the cops through the marsh, where my friend
Donny got hit by a runaway tire from a Ford
Mustang. We jumped off that bridge when
the tide was high, three stories into the cold Atlantic,
until the cops chased us from there too.

When I was eighteen they built a disco on the
other side, Jacob's Ladder. They lined up in tight
white pants and starched hair and dropped black
beauties to the thick bass beats I could hear from
my bedroom window. Now I walk my dog here
when I come to visit my mother, see the fresh

ashes
there?

graffiti that covers our own, see the shopping carts
knee-deep in the low tide mud and the condos,
where a schoolyard used to be, where I played
basketball with no shirt and smoked cigarettes
and stole pieces of pipe from the monkey bars
to make my chopper bicycle, where the guys
played acey-deucey on the schoolyard steps,
and the girls who came to visit for the summer
found eager young boys like a pack of dogs, waiting.

I'm rooted to this place, like the forgotten dancehall
pier, sea-soaked and splintered with each new tide,
this place, once a dumping ground for mob hits,
a revolving door of immigrants, home to the madness
that comes from hot summers and too much booze
and never-ending traffic cruising the three-mile
beachfront boulevard at night.

But once when I was six years old I walked
with my father at low tide, the Nahant beach causeway
on one side, the staggered Boston buildings on the other,
a plane flying low to Logan Airport. We held hands and stepped
over the rigged mounds of packed sand, the scattered
strands of seaweed brushing my ankles, the salt air,
the smell of sun-tan lotion, the seagulls. We walked
to the edge of the channel, the boats an arm's length away,
the neighborhood behind us in the distance. I remember it was late
in the day, the sun hazy and starting down. We stood
looking back at the tiny houses, the neat lined streets,
until the water rose slowly around our legs,
the small cool waves pushing us home, and somewhere out of
sight I heard the faint chimes of an ice-cream truck.

always
at beaches

Movies

When I go to the movies I see me
a black cape over Gotham City _– Batman_
running the rapids in a lost forest
shooting someone in slow motion
or getting shot and dying
to the rising tide of violins.
My son shares this fascination.
He is thirteen and we go to the movies
often together and sometimes,
when we are not whispering to each other,
time freezes in the real world, _– enjoying every minute of life_
ninety minutes turns into years,
but like in Narnia we are still the same,
not getting older too fast,
not getting to the point
where we don't need each other,
not separated by necessity.
For ninety minutes we are both King Kong
or Gandalf or the dwarf in *The Station Agent*.
For ninety minutes we are left holding hands
on our way to see a sunset
in an endless roll of credits.

Memory Boys (high school reunion)

At my reunion I didn't see any of the guys
I really wanted to see
just a lot of high-school kids
dressed up as middle-aged men
hair missing in a variety of places
and bodies reformed into softer shape
but not the kids I remembered, not the boys
from this all boys school
the ones in grass-stained football uniforms
or squeaking sneakers on the floor
of the gymnasium
the ones sneaking cigarettes in the graveyard
down the street from the student union
or flipping butter pads to the ceiling
of the dining hall
all I saw were doctors and bankers
and a country club brat or two
some reliving the glory days
complete with poetic license
some still feeling superior after all these years
putting themselves in the hall of fame
I didn't want to talk so much about sports
or school or families or careers
I wanted to talk about the kid who got drunk my senior year
and scaled the slate roof of the dormitory,
gable to gable, four of them, like Spiderman,
and hopped into the Xavier Hall tower
and rang the bell at three in the morning
with a hunk of steel pipe as if he were Quasimodo
put that motherfucker in the hall of fame.

14

Michaela

You're the one I joke with
about jumping off the cliff
and yelling your name,
"Michaela made me do it,"
the one I still can't get out of bed
in the morning or get to stop
watching *Gilmore Girls*
(even though it sucks me
in too), or get you to clean
the clutter from your dresser
drawers— the used ticket stubs,
the half-finished notebook drawings,
the game shirts you've outgrown.

I'm writing this because
you still need me, but more
because I need that purpose
in my life that never ends,
I need to see you sleeping
and think you are still two
years old,
I need to hold your hand
and pretend you can't
walk without me
or that you need me to show you
how to work a computer,
do the biosphere rocket
in the Math Blaster game
or click the mouse
on the jigsaw puzzle parts.

Shifts from possible girlfriend to daughter

15

We need it all, don't we?
The extra hour of sleep,
the television heroes,
the need to not grow up so fast,
the whole messy drawerful.

everyone
has at least
one messy
drawer

Shredding Me *(from prompt about writing about an object that had some effect on your life)*

I was liberated by my shredder,
a fifteen-page CD-crushing
super-shredder.
I emptied a drawer of old bills,
fed the crisscross steel jaws
with late payments
and a side of overdues
and a dish of slips
marked *paid* with check numbers,
proof of my existence.
I fed that grinding machine
a list of capital expenditures,
credit cards, car insurance,
utility bills, how much water
I used,
how many times I flushed,
how often I bought socks
and underwear and sneakers.
I was liberated from my debt-ridden past
with the simple passage of paper,
memories chewed one hundred times
and swallowed.
So why not, I figured;   — humor
why not these bills,
the ones I haven't payed yet,
the ones due a month from now
(out of sight, out of register).
And if that didn't work
then I would shred the late notices
and the collections and the revocations

and the suit from the bank,
who might come to bulldoze my house,
and even though the shredder warns
about getting your tie caught _more humor_
I'd stuff him in anyway,
squeeze him through the credit-card slot,
the one with the extra-tough teeth,
and I'd shred the cops that came looking
for the bank guy,
cut right through their badges
and their handcuffs.
Remember it's a super-shredder,
chews squad cars and FBI microphones
and uniforms and combat boots
and members of the National Guard
who come looking for chewed-up cops,
who come looking for talking bank heads.
It even shreds tanks and planes
and rocket-propelled missiles,
if they end up wanting my money that bad,
and when I'm finished with my credit history
and any traces of my future debt
I might slip in a few personals,
maybe shred some mistakes I've made,
some laws I've broken,
old lies I told myself,
myths I had created,
perhaps even shred a big idea I had once
that got going all wrong,
and when I was finished with that,
maybe I'd step into the shredder myself,
let those hungry teeth chew my socks,
then my toes,

(sideways looks like shredding paper)

then the bone and the marrow,
let them make me into biodegradable pieces
small red-white bits of me
that could be scattered
around the fields of the world,
like Johnny Appleseed
pulled me from his pouch,
let the wind plant me
firmly in the ground.

Looking In My Neighbor's Yard

I don't think I'll see it move
this summer,
the forty-year-old
wooden-hulled *Bodacious*
won't see it take the corner
on a trailer like the circus
pulling out of town,
maybe shaving a few shreds
off my corner fencepost on the way.
The Captain has Lou Gehrig's disease
and it's eating him quick.
His muscles and his voice
and his days dodging fast-moving storms
are over.
So it sits in the yard
like a statue at the museum,
depicting American summer distractions,
and already the paint is peeling
and the tarp over its head is frayed
and it looks landlocked
and awkward
with the lilac trees blooming around it.

starts with death
and ends with life

After

wine would have been easier I say
wine and a little cheese
maybe some of that rubber pepperoni
from Castiello's
but she only hears every other word
and answers in short quips
like some cryptic form of verse
yup - you go - a little - thanks
and I fix the wheat-bread triangles in a line
resting them on each other
like shingles on a roof
until I hear the cars outside
doors closing and people talking
and I check the cooler for ice
and the coffee pot and the pastries
they sent from the funeral home —turns into sad mood
and the first hand I shake is cool.
~ like death?

Seventh Grade

That was the year we had Miss Mosha for math. She was tall with a big head and always wore something green. I used to see her walking alone on the weekends by the sea wall. That was also the year we got into chewing sheets of notebook paper into jumbo balls of mush so we could spit them on each other. One day I stood to deliver a wet one to Danny Cippoli, head down writing and unsuspecting, and I inhaled (because you needed to get a good wind behind these) and the ball of pulp retreated and stuck in my throat and I made a noise, the kind of noise you make when your windpipe is blocked, and Miss Mosha turned and yelled, "Sit down, Mr. Carey," and I sucked for another breath. "Sit down, now!" she screamed. Perhaps she hadn't noticed that I was a darker shade of red, more beet than my normal white Irish skin, because she yelled again, "Sit down!" But this time I didn't hear it, just saw her big head moving, her lips forming words, the tiny veins in her neck bulging, but no sound, only a dull ringing in my ears, and I drew again for air, the blood rushing to my brain, and for a moment I could see my dog, Red, running on the side lawn after a squirrel, and my feet digging into the wet sand at low tide, and a cotton candy stick at Fenway Park, and then it came, from half way down my esophagus, the promise, the purging, the air returning to my lungs and the white wet missile passing my lips, but nowhere near its target, and Miss Mosha's repeated question like a chant, "What is that? What is that?" and Danny Cippoli's laughter, and the melted marshmallow spreading over the toe of a green high-heeled pump.

For Fitz

Every time I come to New Jersey
I think of you,
the pride of Red Bank,
pushing your father's car
up the street before a game
to work your legs,
that jumpshot frozen
in the local newspaper,
and those nights in the dorm
watching you roll a cigarette
across your knuckles
like a magician's coin,
flicking it to your lips
like the cards you snapped,
tight and spinning to the table,
and the last time we spoke
in the swamp in Florida
after they pulled you from the car   *goes from nice memorys*
and carved out a hunk of your brain   *to "reality"*
and sat you in the corner of a muggy
screened room trying to think
of some story about a spider,
you who played the guitar
and sang and painted and danced,
and dated all the girls we couldn't,
you whom I was always jealous of
nodding off to sleep in a white wicker
chair at noontime and your sister saying,
"He does that a lot."

And that last hot day in Red Bank
when we dropped red roses on your casket

and your mother told us when you died
she said ten Hail Marys at the dining-
room table, and all the way home
I thought of her, hands fixed firmly,
pointing to the ceiling like the nuns taught her,
head bowed over a white linen tablecloth,
her lips whispering the prayer *now and at*
the hour of our death, and the different pieces
of her son running around the room
looking to connect one more time.

Not being able to
let go. Holding on
to every last bit

Loved Hockey

Richy Simmons used to draw
stick figures with big square heads
tumbling down a hillside,
craggy boulders falling after them.
They always had expressions on their faces
like someone had just given them a Christmas
present, an alarm clock or a pair of sneakers,   *~ great way to explain it*
a look that said, *Thanks, just what I always wanted.*
He'd pass me the drawings in math class,
show me the arrow pointing to a teacher's name
from one of the stick bodies pinned under a rock
then he'd laugh until the spittle formed
on the corners of his mouth.
He always drew the hair on their heads
like tiny spikes, resembling
the constant crewcut his police-chief father
made him get.
Once he hung onto the window of the bus
as it took off around the corner,
hanging there like a man on a cliff,
finally falling when it got going too fast
and rolling into the hedges on Tobin Street
by the river that ran under
the General Edwards Bridge,
but that was way before   *} mood shift*
he started selling crack
from a tiny Revere Beach condo
where he shot homemade porno movies
with the girls from Shirley Ave.

25

Before he died at thirty years old
and everyone said, *I told you so*.

But for a long time he loved hockey,
loved skating on the frozen river
in the winter,
handling the puck in the street,
loved the Bruins and the Montreal
Canadiens, loved playing
wiffleball in his backyard,
setting the boundaries
and the bases, loved drawing
pictures and telling jokes,
loved riding his bicycle
around the point and watching
the train disappear by the marsh road,
but even back then there was
a cloud around him, maybe
because his father and his
brother beat him up too much,
or maybe because the kids on
Riverside talked him into
something stupid every day,
like latching onto a moving bus.
Even then it seemed like he was
waiting for the avalanche,
waiting for life to roll itself
into solid balls of aged earth,
come raining down on the tiny
spikes of his head.

from death to his loving life

Man on the Beach

I watch the man in the leather jacket
smoking a cigarette against the sea wall,
a slice of graffiti cut off in mid-thought.
He seems disturbed by my presence,
the smoke around him like an aura
of gray dusk, a few empty beer cans at his feet.
He doesn't know I once walked this beach
with a pocket full of quarters to play skee ball,
saw a boy with an eye patch dropping
a switchblade into an empty beer bottle,
doesn't know my uncle would have gotten shot
tending bar if he hadn't run to the racetrack,
or that my friend Donny was killed by a car
crossing the boulevard a hundred yards from here.
Maybe he would agree with me if I said,
"The beach makes strangers of us all."

The water at the man's back is more blue
this time of year, the sand less white than summer,
the same loud motorcycles cruising up and down,
the same neon lights jumping out of the twilight:
to drink, to dance, to eat.
He flicks his cigarette to the ground
and walks away and I want to tell him
there is no where on the beach he can hide,
not against the crumbling sea walls,
or in the glow of honky-tonk lights,
or behind the screen of sea smoke
that dances off the cold blue water in winter.

Out the Office Window

It's one of those nights
at the end of the summer
and the promise of autumn
blows cool in the breeze
and the sun sets orange
over the triple-decker rooftops
and the trees and the seagulls
heading for the beach
and a kid rides his bike
through the empty parking lot
drinking a can of soda
and the headlights from the cars
on Cabot Street reflect
off a window across the way
like tiny Christmas bulbs
and a guy plays a saxophone
out a second-floor corner window
a cool jazz riff I can barely hear
over the exhaust fan on the roof
but I know it's there, cause I see him
and I hear it blow in the back of my mind
like a memory or a voice
in between the whir of fan blades
and it soothes the sound of the city
and the end of summer
and the cool fall days approaching.

So much out of just one window

Uncle Paul

I remember him when he was a bartender,
a white rag tucked into his back pocket,
bowlegged, smoking, stories about the Navy
and how he could roll a rubber tire
thirty feet and make it turn around
and come back to him,
before the cancer, not once, but twice,
and all after he stopped going to
the racetrack sober and became
his own best customer again.   *Showing, not telling*
I remember the night some wise guy
shot up the bar and killed his friend Ray
while he was playing the daily double,
the night my mother told us
to pray and go back to bed.
I remember him cracking a joke
in the detox hallway when
I took him there with my father.
He was smiling as he checked in
as if he'd rented a penthouse with a pool.

                    *unaware
                      of
                        real life*

Eighth Grade

That was the year I played freshman basketball
even though I was in the eighth grade,
went to Washington, D.C., and had an appendix
attack in front of Abraham Lincoln,
felt up Liz Shea on the bus ride home,
the year we smoked pot on the catwalk
of the G.E. Bridge and played spin the bottle
in the basement of the church,
the year the kids sniffed model glue
from plastic bags in the back of the bus
and Tom Ferragamo threw a desk at me
and dented the chalkboard behind my head,
the year they boxed my ears in English class
and got me to fight even though I didn't want to,
the year Mossy Lynch the gangster
gave me twenty bucks at Christmas
and Muzzy Terminello, who weighed
three hundred pounds and never let us use
the phone booth at the drugstore, ended up
in the trunk of a car with five bullet holes in his head,
the same year I got caught drinking beer
I'd stolen from my brother-in-law's cookout
and started working the beach,
making onion rings with white and yellow
flour, coming home smelling like cornmeal
and canola, the year Joe Cody returned
from the war and did a headstand on a telephone pole,
and Bob Dellripa, who could imitate anybody
and spent a whole month speaking like John Wayne,
got hit and killed walking home on the railroad tracks
while his father, his only parent, was off flying planes.

30

Red Sneakers

you stole my red sneakers and boxed my ears
in English class
and never said a word,
not even years later
when I saw you drinking rum by a pool table,
or years after that
in line for takeout food on the beach
one hot July night.
You looked tired and confused and sick
and I remembered thinking I'd outlasted you,
and our eyes met and you nodded your head
as if I were a traffic cop,
a paper boy,
a bartender,
someone put in place to get you by.

role reversal

Atomic Café

A cup of tea so big it's half cold on the table,
a pile of World Lit papers in front of me,
Gilgamesh, Enkidu and the original flood story
(fifteen hundred years before the other one),
and a table full of bottled redheads
and students from the college
talking about God or Saturday night
and out the window a tattooed woman with her baby,
a thirty-year-old gangster in an army cap,
a teenage girl in shorts on a bike by the Cabot Theater,
and for a moment I forget where I have to be,
for ten minutes I don't think about dying
or the void of the afterlife
or the reason for not living without worry
or fear or having something to do always,
and a van pulls up and a few guys in overalls
empty out to paint somewhere
and the gangster hugs a girl in a summer dress
with rings through her body
and the baby plays with her mother's painted wrists
and I look at another Gilgamesh essay
the need to be recognized or
four thousand year's worth of killing time.

tattoos
or
slits

Action

My son reads a film magazine in the lobby
of the Kendall Square Cinema
waiting to see a French martial
arts movie, the less melodramatic kind,
like my wife tells me my writing used to be.
About fifty-five guys get killed
in the first few minutes
but it's beautifully choreographed
and the two leads share spectacular kicks
and run up walls and leap from the roofs
of buildings after each other
and it's the way it should be,
the good and the brave outlasting the evil
and nobody gets the girl until she says so.

We drive home talking in spurts
about the sound track and the style
and how one bad guy comes off
not so bad even though he kills three
people in cold blood in the first thirty
seconds, and the air is not as hot as it was
so I kill the A.C. and open my window
and rest my arm against the night breeze
and shift gears to pass a white van
full of dark windows
and drive a little faster than I normally do.

Running

The children yell from the schoolyard
in little blue pants and white shirts
and kick a big red ball between them
like a pinball game and it doesn't seem
that long ago: playing kickball or ring-a-levio
or running over the buckled hot top
to catch a rubber pimple ball,
not so long ago when I skinned
my knees running on the sidewalk
and cried looking in the mirror
because my chin bled red,
my blood darker now
when I nick myself shaving   ~ from kickball
like even that has aged.   to adult hood
I turned fifty this year and a half
a century seems like a history
lesson, like someone should be
answering an essay question about
my childhood for extra credit,
or scanning my homework written in
longhand as some withered yellow parchment,
and wasn't it true that the trees
grew taller then in my backyard
and we built snow forts as big
as apartment buildings,
but my grandmother lived to be
ninety-nine and in the end smiled
with no teeth and wrapped pennies
up in napkins that she tucked into
her sleeves. That's forty-nine more years

for me, a lifetime if you consider
my friend Fitzy, dead at thirty-six from
a brain tumor, or three lifetimes if
you think about Kenny Percell,
crossing the highway after a paper route.
The children at the schoolyard run like I used to
before a knee injury, run for the bases,
from getting tagged by the big red ball,
run from getting punched when
the nuns aren't looking. They run
instinctively as if what they're
running from is lurking around every corner.

 — Running from death

White Mountains

Six years
and the brittle branches
of the mountain conifers
still rise and shrink
with each slow step,
this place, changeless and
frozen and waiting for me;
the sounds still ringing in my ears,
the chatter of passing hikers
the hush of thirty eighth-graders
being told Manhattan is under attack.

Six years and still they hide
like burrowed brown ticks
beneath my skin,
things we couldn't see yet:
crowds of people running,
clouds of black smoke,
candles burning on the trunks of cars,
draped flag after draped flag
on the quiet highway home.

We had wished for phones
and families,
for televisions and newspapers,
for cable news and the Internet,
wished to know the things
we didn't want to know. ~ Such a true
statement

Six years and still I remember
what I was thinking;
I was thinking that these mountains
once erupted out of ash,
out of chaos,
these stone stacks of time
once as brittle as the buildings we erect,
as perpetual as the dreams of architects,
as comforting as a sunny day
and the promise of a flight home,

the oath we take with things eternal
as if nothing ever happens.

Kay

You were never my girlfriend,
not even in your mind,
not the one I almost married
after a drunk night on Nantaskett Beach
and stayed with for two years.
But it's you I remember,
The jeans you wore, smoking
pot from that purple elephant bong,
and the night we scraped up
twenty bucks in change and walked
a mile and a half to Lietrim's
and tossed it on the bar and asked
Dave to make it last and split your
last pack of Newports. And later
walking back and knocking on the door
of the church and being turned away
by a priest in his nightclothes,
and at one point you caught up to me
and held my hand and we stopped talking
and walked that way for a mile or so,
the cool touch of your skin, the firm clench
of your fingers, and I think I would have
held it forever if you had asked me to.

Winter Coming

In my town they'll run you
over on the crosswalk
if you get in the way
of the morning commute,
not as bad as some parts
of New Jersey, I suppose,
where they'll run you over
all day long.
I'm not paying attention
when I cross the street,
I'm looking at the leaves falling
and finding it odd
that when everything is dying
I'm thinking of beginning again;
when everything outside is dark
and cold and gray
I'm comforted by the gloom.
I wonder if it's like shedding skin,
or starting over after confession,
and I don't see the car
honking at me.
I'm the absent-minded fool
crossing the street with his coffee,
looking at the trees, digesting
the promise of white-powdered
sidewalks and low full moons
and the cold crisp air returning.

Thinking of Wallace Stevens on a Saturday Morning in Hartford

A statue of someone looking stately
and European outside the Atheneum,
green and bronze, a bird on the hand.
The warm July breeze is slight,
people changing buses,
taking their time past the few high-rise
buildings reflecting copper images
of the empty streets,
like warped funhouse mirrors,
the beige brick, the pale mortar,
a generator whining alone somewhere.
It's shady here and I wonder if Stevens
sat writing a poem,
a women clicking her heels behind him,
a fountain bubbling,
a child crying in her mother's arms,
everything hushed and pregnant
and waiting.

Crossing the Tappan Zee Bridge

Every time I cross the Tappan Zee
I choose a song carefully as if
I'm in a movie, the main character
leaving home after college, or breaking
up with his girlfriend and driving away,
or maybe just starting over somehow.
It could be the beginning of the movie
or the end; the song is a ballad, I think,
not jazz, something with lyrics at least,
Lucinda Williams or Steve Earl or R.E.M.
I think it's a P.O.V shot, me watching
the traffic beyond the windshield
panning side to side to see the city,
or the sand cliffs in Nyack. Maybe one shot
of the girders over head, then closing
the sequence with a helicopter tracking
from a few hundred yards, a big shot,
one that lets the audience feel
what they're in for, gives them a chance
to think about the scene before,
and then it's over and I'm on Route 95
and nothing feels the same
or as interesting and I realize it's only my movie
and I've got hours left to drive.

A Summer Day on White Pond

for Wang Wei

The breeze blew warm
through the pale leaves
of the skinny white birch trees,
carried the scent of my father's tanning oil,
the hum of a transistor radio.

I chased a frog from the cover
of wild weeds, squeezed him tight
as he jumped from my fingers
to the cool dark water around my legs.

And a rowboat passed by
sending ripples to the shore,
an old man from across the lake
rolling an oar in each hand, left then right,
smiling and recognizing
just how hard they are to hold.

The Things We Do

I grew up playing basketball
on a backyard court my father
hot-topped, shooting from
the painted free-throw line,
pretending I was a Boston Celtic,
Sam Jones, too late!

My father watched from the kitchen
window in those days, me and the kids
from the neighborhood playing
two on two, hot summer afternoons,
shirtless, sweating, drinking water
from the garden hose.

Every time I was involved with
basketball he was there,
sitting in the stands,
driving me to gymnasiums all over
the state, coming up with Celtics tickets
on a Sunday afternoon, the third-floor
Garden doors open, the banners
hanging against the smoky ceiling.

It was like we played the game together,
as if any success I had
was a direct result of his wishing it,
his praying for it, maybe. It was harder
for him than me when the coach decided
to cut my playing time and the desire to
play the game evaporated and the politics

of high school sports left him fighting for
my minutes in the lobby of the gymnasium.

But that one night in Boston Garden,
when I came cold off the bench
and made two free throws to seal
a tournament game, he waited for me
outside the bus in the rain,
his trench coat soaked, his soft hat dripping,
and he hugged me and held me a little
longer than usual, and when he wanted
to talk more about it, to share in
the victory after many years of watching
from the kitchen window, or the dusty bleachers,
when he wanted to take me to dinner I said,
"There's a party at the coach's house."

"You go," he told me. "Have fun."
And I did and he drove home in silence,
thinking of the game, I'm sure, of the two
free throws he willed in from the seats,
thinking of something like redemption,
the raindrops collecting on the seat around him
from the wet brim of his hat.

Coyote's Lament (cartoon)

Do you know what it's like
knowing you will never win?
The predetermined cloud
hanging over your head
like a death knell,
reaching repeatedly for
the very thing you can't get,
the ring on the carousel
inches from your outstretched
fingers over and over again
or setting the perfect trap
on the same dusty road day after day
the preparation, the planning, the care,
then what? A boulder falling out of
nowhere, another mechanical malfunction,
a jagged cliff cut in half and you fall
from a cloudless sky one more time,
a lifeless poof of smoke in the dead
canyon below and he, the rubber-neck
dolt, gets to run and run, brainless
and euphoric and loud and obnoxious
like some hapless puppy prancing
through the day, never responsible,
never worrying, never afraid?
What's the reward for thinking,
for reasoning, for seeking answers
and solutions?
Beep beep. Ignorance is bliss.
You'd think they'd have pity
just one Saturday morning.

Worcester

To this day I remember the ride we took
in your blue box car, winding down
Salisbury Street, past the trimmed lawns
and the clean swept driveways.
Did you sleep with him?

I had you let me out by the duck pond
where redheaded Neil drowned a few
months later. (The gang jumped in
in their underwear and he died
right there while they ran back up the hill.)

When you drove away I was alone
and I remember thinking I'd find Walshie,
maybe smoke a bone,
play some Roy Buchanan and crash
on the townhouse couch.

Thirty years later and still I can see the gray
Worcester sky, the empty Sunday campus,
the way the lily pads float
into groups on the dark pond water,
like bathers quietly gossiping.

Mother Told Me

My mother once told me
to keep my penis in my pants.
I know she didn't mean
all the time; I know

she meant when Regina Armstrong
wanted to show me her underwear
or when that girl Laurie who lived
on the point told me jokes about the womb.

Or maybe she meant the nights
we bought quart bottles of beer
and pissed on car tires or wrote
our initials on the street with our urine.

So many ways to get in trouble
when you let that thing out,
she probably figured, never mind
what you could come home with—

V.D., herpes (even then) or, worse,
a baby. Somebody else's baby.
Or maybe she meant when I was alone,
when they'd go out for dinner

at the Red Coach Grill
and I'd take too long in the bathroom.
Maybe she wanted to keep me
from going blind.

What if I did keep it in my pants
all those years? Would I be better off?
Those times in college,
those nights on the beach?

Eventually I took her advice,
worked two jobs, had two kids,
racked up fagged-out hours every night,
changing diapers, cleaning puke,
singing lullabies until I fell asleep.

In those years it felt more like
an antique car parked in the garage
with a tarp over it, waiting to come out
for the Fourth of July parade.

— great Comparison

Basketball

I don't play so much anymore
but I coach seventh graders—
how to make a layup, break
a half-court trap, play a 2-3 zone.
It's different from the days
in high school when I lived
for it, shoveled snow from my
backyard court to shoot around
all winter, summer camps, state
tournaments in Boston Garden.
Now it's more about helping kids
to feel good about playing
or sometimes keeping them from
killing each other, like last week
when a redheaded kid punched someone
and I asked why and he said, "Do you
want to know what he called
me?" and I said, "Yes, what did
he call you?" and he said, "Fire
nuts," and I realized then that
coaching has little to do with
basketball and more to do with
not laughing at the wrong moment.
Yet I still remember what it was
like to get a new ball
every Christmas morning,
still remember my father's voice
in the stands, still remember two
free throws in a state tournament
game, still remember weekends playing

at the YMCA, where Pete Pedro
called us yardbirds for showering
with our bathing suits on, and the
schoolyard where I played for hours
and hours, where I felt safe, where
I fit in, where the names they
came up with didn't matter.

Out of Sight

I watched a hawk one day
flying high over the bare brown
trees of a forest,
beat beat glide
beat beat glide.
I watched for a long time
while it veered and dipped and dove
in the pockets of white clouds,
in the fading blue dusk,
watched until it was just a line
in the darkening sky,
then a speck or a trace
or something I might have seen,
something missing but living
just beyond my sight.
Maybe that's where they go, I thought,
my Uncle Paul,
my yellow lab mutt,
my favorite bartender,
my high school basketball coach,
my neighbor's baby,
my dad,
all of them hunkered down,
just out of sight,
waiting to be remembered.

Realizing a Dream

Last night another big one fell.
I felt the shudder in the foundation
as I lay under bags of sand
with my sister.
This one hit three counties over
wiped out a mini-mall, a school,
and three farmhouses.
No one is worried about the economy
anymore,
no wars to fight, no enemies to
recognize,
just the universe folding in on
itself.
When the next one comes
I might grab my baseball glove
track it down like an outfielder
in the night sky,
make a basket catch in some empty
open field.
Anything is better than the waiting.

Acknowledgments

Thanks to those who have taught me much about writing poetry: Salem State University faculty members Rod Kessler and J. D. Scrimgeour, Salem Writers Group, January O'Neil, Colleen Michaels, Jennifer Jean, the crew at The Nunnery: Maria Mazziotti Gillan, Laura Boss, Mark Hillringhouse, Bob Evans, the Fairleigh Dickinson MFA program and faculty members David Daniel and Bill Zander. Also thanks to Ed Boyle, Jack Highberger, Tim Young, my wife, Betty, and my kids, Kevin and Michaela, for their conversation, inspiration, and support. And special thanks to Baron Wormser and Dawn Potter for their editorial wisdom.

Several of the poems in this collection were previously published, some in a slightly different form, in the following journals:

Comstock Review: "A Well-Oiled Machine"

Endicott Review: "Uncle Paul."

Lips: "Crazy Stuff"

The Paterson Literary Review: "Basketball," "for Fitz," "Frozen Peas," "Loved Hockey," "Memory Boys," "Michaela," "Mother Told Me," "Movies," "The One-Fifteen to Penn Station," "Revere Beach" "The Road Narrows," "Seventh Grade"

Sexton Magazine: "Running."

The White Pelican Review: "Looking in My Neighbor's Yard," "Shredding Me."

Xanadu: "Out of Sight"

Other Books in the New Voices Series

CavanKerry's Mission

Through publishing and programming, CavanKerry Press connects communities of writers with communities of readers. We publish poetry that reaches from the page to include the reader, by the finest new and established contemporary writers. Our programming brings our books and our poets to people where they live, cultivating new audiences and nourishing established ones.